The Elephant's Trunk

Story by Lynn Salem and Josie Stewart
Illustrations by Kristi Gerner

The elephant's trunk is his hand.
He picks leaves to eat.

A baby can't eat with his trunk.

Soon a baby can hold his mother's tail with his trunk.

Elephants blow dirt and water from their trunks to keep cool.

And elephants can breathe underwater with their trunks!